This book belongs to:

....

....

....

Also by Sarah Rayner

Non-fiction:
Making Friends with Anxiety
Making Friends with the Menopause

Fiction:
Another Night, Another Day
The Two Week Wait
One Moment, One Morning
Getting Even
The Other Half

Children's books written and illustrated
by Jules Miller:

Ellie and the truth about the Tooth Fairy
When Night Became Day

Making Friends with Anxiety: A Calming Colouring Book

Words by SARAH RAYNER
Pictures by JULES MILLER

Inspiring words and pictures designed to ease worry and panic

ISBN-978-1514190098

www.thecreativepumpkin.com
www.julesmiller.uk

Hello and welcome to our colouring-in book

I'm **Sarah Rayner,** and my day (and sometimes night) job is as an author. Some of you may know my novels which include *One Moment, One Morning* and *The Two Week Wait*, or you might have come across this via my non-fiction book, *Making Friends with Anxiety: A warm, supportive little book to help ease worry and panic*, which – to my delight – has been a word-of-mouth success. If you liked that, I hope you'll enjoy this too: it's similar, but different. *Making Friends with Anxiety: A Calming Colouring Book* focuses on creative activities and explains how they can help us be less anxious, together with pictures by the illustrator **Jules Miller.**

'But there are other books on anxiety!' we hear you cry. 'And lots of other colouring books too! What makes yours so special?' Well, when it comes to anxiety, the answer is simple: 'We've both been there.'

Jules and I have been friends for nearly 20 years. We met in an ad agency, where we worked together as a copywriter and art director, and the pressures of advertising – with its tight deadlines and demanding clients – are intense. We've both suffered from the effects of stress, and whilst we can't promise to cure your anxiety (that would be an over-claim for any book to make) nonetheless, over the years we have learned to manage our anxiety by 'making friends' with it. This approach has already helped thousands of readers of the first *Making Friends with Anxiety* book, and now we're delighted to share our skills and experience here.

As for instructions, there aren't any!

With this calming colouring-in book, the idea is to let your imagination run free so you colour each beautiful picture exactly as you choose. We'll give you a few tips on methods and materials a bit further on, but we don't want using this book to feel like a lesson or a task. We've deliberately kept the price point low to make it affordable to as many readers as possible and you don't need to have read the other *Making Friends with Anxiety* book or have great colouring skills. Ultimately, all you need is some coloured pens, pencils or crayons and a little time. The very act of colouring is so relaxing you'll soon find yourself in an almost meditative state – perhaps it's because it brings out a childlike joy in each of us – and that's the first step to easing worry and panic right there.

What also makes this book special is that each picture incorporates a 'mantra' – a few words with psychological power. These mantras will help further sustain and comfort you, and when these words and pictures are combined with your colouring… that's when the real magic happens. Each then becomes a unique work of art designed to boost your mood whenever you look at it. You may want to put up your favourites in your home or workplace (in which case cut the pages out along the dotted lines) or you might prefer to keep the book handy so you can dip into it should you have a wobbly day.

In addition, you might like to join the *Making Friends with Anxiety Facebook Group,* (www.facebook.com/groups/makingfriendswithanxiety/) which provides a space for anxiety sufferers to share experiences and support one another in confidence. You could post your pictures there too, though there is no pressure to do so. Whatever, we hope you find this colouring-in book helps unlock your creativity and confidence and brings greater calm and contentment into your life.

Sarah & Jules

Anxiety affects us all

Let's kick off with an assertion: that *you*, dear reader, are anxious. I can say this not just because this book has got 'anxiety' in the title and you're choosing to read it, but because **everyone is anxious in some way.**

'But I know lots of people who never seem to worry about anything,' you might counter. 'They sail through life with a *la di da* and nothing ever fazes them.' I get where you're coming from. Take someone like the Dalai Lama – he seems a very mellow fellow, so how can I make such a sweeping statement? Admittedly, I've no idea if the Dalai Lama tosses and turns at night or bites his nails in secret, but I'd still assert that His Holiness experiences anxiety. Moreover, **there's nothing wrong with this.** This is because anxiety is just as common and natural an emotion as happiness and sadness, love and compassion. So unless the Dalai Lama simply isn't human, he'll experience anxiety to some degree, and I don't know about you, but I find just knowing this is comforting.

The problem is that **some people experience *heightened* anxiety.** Personally, I'm nowhere near as bad as I was, but I'd still put myself in worrywart club. At various times anxiety has meant I've been unable to work, interfered with my relationships and zapped my confidence. Jules' anxiety has never been quite this bad, but it's still been crushing on occasion, and you can probably place yourself somewhere on a scale which has Jules and me close to one end and our Tibetan friend at the other.

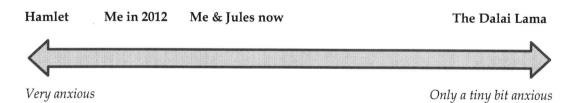

Hamlet   Me in 2012   Me & Jules now   The Dalai Lama

Very anxious   *Only a tiny bit anxious*

The Gardener's Retreat

Step by step you can befriend anxiety

"Therein lies the rub..."

...as Hamlet (who knew a thing or two about fretting) would say. If anxiety is a perfectly natural emotion, why does it dominate the lives of some of us in particular? Panic attacks, OCD, Post Traumatic Stress – however it manifests itself, anxiety can be very distressing when we're in its thrall. I could theorise about how we live in a particularly anxiety-provoking age where work emails and social networking and worries about debt and climate change jostle for our headspace 24/7, so it's no wonder we're near crazy. But there are numerous essays and articles on that already. Let's cut to the chase so we can get going with the Crayola. Instead you'll find:

- A summary of **what happens physically when we get anxious**
- An explanation of **why some of us are prone to heightened, Hamlet-like levels of worry and fear**
- **Five ways to start making friends with anxiety** right away
- An exploration of **why colouring can be so good at soothing and de-stressing us**
- A look at **why other activities** like needlework, gardening and being with animals **work in a similar calming way**
- Finishing up with **some gentle encouragement about facing anxiety** to help you on your onward journey

Throughout you'll find tried-and-tested tips from members of the *Making Friends with Anxiety Facebook Group,* many of whom have acquired great wisdom as a result of their own experience of fear and panic. We want this book to have as positive an impact on how you feel as possible, and by the end we hope you've a palette of options to choose from in terms of managing your own worry and stress as well as some lovely pictures to put on the wall.

So what happens physically when we experience anxiety?

It might surprise you to discover that anxiety isn't a bad thing per se. In many ways it can actually serve us. This is because **anxiety is connected to fear.*** It could be said that anxiety is the biological vestige of fear, the basic survival mechanism that helps safeguard us against danger. **When we experience fear, we get a rush of adrenaline.**

- The brain sends a biochemical message saying 'all systems go!' and **our breathing becomes faster and shallower,** supplying more oxygen to the muscles.
- **Our hearts beat more rapidly and blood is driven to the brain and limbs** so we can make split-second decisions and a quick getaway. This is why when we are anxious we often experience heart palpitations, chest pains and tingling.
- **Blood is taken from areas of the body where it's not needed,** such as the stomach, because in a life-threatening situation, you're not going to stop for food. So when you're afraid, you may well feel sick and be unable to eat.
- **The liver releases stored sugar to provide fuel for quick energy.** Excess sugar in the blood can cause indigestion.
- **Muscles in the anus and bladder are relaxed.** Food and liquid are evacuated so you're lighter in order to run. Hence diarrhoea and frequent urination.
- **The body cools itself by perspiring.** Blood vessels and capillaries move close to the skin surface, leading to sweating and blushing.

Thus what can seem like horribly frightening symptoms are actually normal biological reactions – the same reactions our ancestors have had for thousands of years.

* I explained this in the first *Making Friends with Anxiety* book, but I promised you wouldn't need to read that to benefit from this, so if you have read that, please bear with this brief recap. There's lots of new information coming up, I promise!

Fear is natural and useful

Fear is natural, that's fact number one. Fact number two is that we need fear, however horrible it feels to be afraid. Imagine you were being threatened by an aggressive animal. Here the burst of adrenaline would bring about a much-needed 'fight or flight' response, useful if you needed to escape from a hungry lion. We can often see our pets exhibit these responses. This very morning, when our cat clapped eyes on the basket in which he goes to the vet, he bolted out of the cat flap faster than a horse on Derby day, and he's not normally a swift mover, take it from me. Fear prompted flight, and it took an awful lot of patience (and a sachet of Whiskas) to lure him back inside.

Whilst you might not encounter hungry lions on a daily basis, **the good thing about anxiety is that it can help alert us to the fact we might be taking too much on and that we have to look after ourselves.** So we need anxiety, just as we need laughter and tears and friends and family; it keeps us safe and healthy. The bad thing is that in some of us, fear gets triggered very easily, resulting in too much adrenaline, and an ongoing anxious state of mind – that Hamlet-like headspace I mentioned. Anxiety is the body signalling something is not quite right, and if we experience this series of reactions in a normal situation such as in a super-market or business meeting, it can be very frightening. **We then become afraid of certain situations and people, and often end up creating a vicious circle** where we avoid many things because they trigger what we interpret as a negative reaction. I'll come back to the subject of avoidance later, at the end of this little book.

TIP: 'If I feel wound up, I go for a walk. It seems to use up my adrenaline, and after a while the brain seems to clear and problems don't feel so overwhelming.' **Peter**

How do we befriend anxiety?

It was on a course on anxiety management that I finally grasped anxiety was a natural response so to try and banish it from my life was as futile as trying to get rid of my appetite or ability to sneeze. I now understand that anxiety is as much a part of me as they are. But it wasn't always this way. Like many people, I concluded anxiety was what was stopping me from being happy and fulfilled, so I fought it, seeing it as the enemy.

Without wanting to sound evangelical or simplistic, if you suffer from excess worry, high levels of stress or panic attacks, I'm a firm believer that **befriending anxiety is *the* key to feeling better. Fighting anxiety, or avoiding trigger situations won't help in the long run. At its most basic, this means changing our mind-set from one of resistance to acceptance.** It's not always easy to change how we think, but **here are five ways to manage anxiety that you can start implementing today:**

1. **Try not to focus so much on the future**

   I've noticed many members of the *Making Friends with Anxiety Facebook Group* expend a lot of mental energy fearing what is yet to happen, and I have the same tendency myself. Going back to work in a week's time, meeting the in-laws in a fortnight, having to fly next month – if you're prone to anxiety, I'm sure you can fill in your own panic-provoking scenarios. Yet most of these are beyond our control and **worrying serves no purpose other than to trigger adrenaline and a raft of physical symptoms.** Personally, I find it impossible not to worry at all, but when I have a lot to do, I break my anxieties down into a list of what I have to accomplish on that day and NO MORE THAN THAT. I ignore everything else and tell myself I will deal with tomorrow when I get there.

2. Stop overthinking everything

To help achieve this, I channel my inner cat – but channelling your inner dog, guinea pig or mouse will do just as well. This isn't as bonkers as it sounds. When other mammals experience fear and have a rush of adrenaline, they don't analyse their symptoms – a cat being chased by a large dog doesn't pause to evaluate 'why is Buster being so aggressive today, is it something I've done?' He just high tails it. At its simplest, this is because our pets live in the present. A cat is happy: it purrs. A dog wants you to throw a ball: it comes running up, wagging its tail. Neither creature (unless I'm missing something) is worried about work on Monday. They just are as they are. Hungry, playful, growly, hot, sleepy. They express it and move on. When we follow their example and let go of ruminating on the past and worrying about the future and focus on the here and now, anxiety lessens.

TIP: *'Know that you have come through anxiety before and you will again.*
You are a survivor.' **Alan**

3. Make contact with nature

Every day take five minutes to experience the great outdoors. Wherever you are, be unashamedly sensual – smell the flowers, gaze at the sky, touch the dewy grass, listen to the birds. Again, this will bring you into the present moment.

TIP: *'I spend a lot of my time drawing plants and I'll often pick one or two flower heads from the garden and place them in a jar by my desk to study close up. Flowers such as pansies and lilies have such amazing and intricate details, yet we often overlook them because we usually see them in busy flower beds and complicated floral displays. Why not spend a few moments looking at the structure of a flower as if though a macro len?*
You'll be amazed at what you'll discover. ' **Jules**

4.   **Exercise – but do what you enjoy**

Physical exercise helps anxiety as it uses up adrenaline and encourages the production of happy hormones. But there's no point joining a gym just because magazines or well-meaning friends tell you to, as if you don't use your membership this will merely create anxiety and guilt. You're better off gardening or dancing or walking the dog. Are you noticing a theme here…? It's called **Do What Makes You Happy.**

5.   **Kiss good-bye to strict diets**

Unless you've an issue with obesity, if you experience heightened anxiety, I think it's a good idea to give up giving up until you're on a more even keel. The symptoms of anxiety will ease gradually if you learn to manage it. Meanwhile, stop dieting, and you'll avoid all that resentment and self-reproach that often goes with counting calories or weighing yourself all the time. Keeping your blood sugar levels stable and avoiding too much caffeine and alcohol will help your anxiety no end, but I believe 'a little bit of what you fancy' doesn't tend to do much harm. One latte a day is probably OK; five isn't. Same with chocolate and cake, coke, wine and beer. **Balance is key.**

TIP: 'Talk to your anxiety in a positive way, as if you are greeting your friend. I do it and as I chat, I can feel my physical symptoms ease. If I build on this positive reaction, it's amazing how quickly my anxiety settles.' **Ellen**

TIP: 'I've got a donkey! When that doubting voice is nagging away, I pretend that it's the donkey from Shrek. I picture him sitting on my shoulder and he makes me smile.' **Alan**

Why colouring can help

According to the Mental Health Foundation, 59% of adults say they are more stressed today than they were five years ago, and it seems the world and his proverbial wife are reaching for their colouring pencils or brush pens in a bid to feel calm. Colouring can help befriend anxiety:

- **...by enabling us to stop focusing on the past** (which is often associated with depression) **and future** (a common tendency of the over-anxious) **and be in the here and now.**
- **...because it is "mind-fullness" made manifest. The mind is filled with an activity which helps stop us overthinking.** We are not able to dissect or churn over anything else when we are concentrating on colouring as, contrary to common belief, it isn't actually possible to think of two things exactly the same time. Instead what happens is the mind darts from one to another, and it is at this which leaves us feeling frazzled and intellectually dissatisfied.

TIP: 'Remember nothing lasts forever, including anxiety. Even if it can seem as if you will never feel good again, bad times will pass, because every emotion is temporary.' **Lucy**

TIP: 'Whenever my head becomes filled with chatter, I write down a list of worries. I then tick off the things I have the power to change – and draw a red line though the things that are out of my control at that time. This way I'm able to separate the 'what if?' fears from life's 'need to do!' demands. I'm always amazed at how much better makes me feel.' **Jules**

Colouring can help reduce the production of adrenaline

Colouring is not a passive act: we need to make creative decisions about which colour to choose and as we focus on not going over the lines, our minds and bodies become more relaxed. Relaxation lowers the activity of the amygdala, a part of the brain that is affected by stress. Thus many of the **physical responses that stem from the release of adrenaline are diminished when we colour:** heart rate slows, breathing becomes less frenetic, blood flows to the stomach so food can be digested more easily – the list goes on. And as we become physically less charged, so our thinking becomes less panicky, and vice versa. The result is that colouring can help turn the vicious circle where anxiety begets more anxiety into a benign one that promotes calm.

TIP: *'If I feel anxious before I set about colouring, I do a little deep breathing. I breathe in for the count of four, hold my breath for the count of seven, then release to the count of eight. I repeat this until I feel my heartbeat slow. This stops me absorbing the worries of a bad day and allows me to use the disassociation that comes from colouring to full advantage. Works every time for me!'* **Amanda**

TIP: *'Adding colour to a black and white illustration in a colouring book can very often feel daunting. Try experimenting with your colour combinations on a blank piece of paper before you work on your finished piece.'* **Jules**

'It's not what you look at that matters, it's what you see.'
Henry David Thoreau

Colouring makes us feel small, in a good way

Is colouring a pastime you remember from your childhood? (I do!) Perhaps you have children and they do it now. In either case, whilst colouring means we don't ruminate as much on the past, in many ways **it allows us as adults to become children once more.** There's something reassuring and comforting about picking up real pens and paper again – especially when our lives are so dominated by screens and mice and keyboards. George Bernard Shaw said, 'we don't stop playing because we grow old, we grow old because we stop playing'.

In our enthusiasm for colouring, however, let's not kid ourselves that we are the first generation to dream up art therapy. One of the first psychiatrists to see how drawing might aid self-exploration was the great Swiss thinker, Carl Jung. In the early 20th century he did this through mandalas – designs which use concentric lines and circles and have their origins in India. He saw them as **'the psychological expression of the totality of the self'** and since then research has provided some backing for his theory. Infants are born with a desire to look at circles, probably because the ability to seek out circular, face-like stimuli helps them to bond with their care givers. For a baby, a circle will come forward out of a confusing mass of random visual input and be recognized as something known and familiar.

TIP: 'I find colouring mandalas or sitting quietly on my own reading Tarot cards very calming. Both these help me visualize what's going on at a deeper level.' **Catherine**

'Nobody is bored when he is trying to make something that is beautiful.'
William Ralph Inge

Colouring this book – paints, pens or pencils?

When it comes to choosing how to colour the pictures in this book, we don't want to be prescriptive and cause you to worry about your approach being 'wrong' in some way. **This is _your_ book and you're free to use it exactly as you please.** If you want to colour the sea pink and fish blue in the picture opposite, then feel free! Nonetheless if you haven't already selected which implements to use and you're new to colouring or haven't done any in a while, here are a few pros and cons of the different media to help steer you:

- **Crayons are fast and convenient** but can be imprecise and result in white spaces.
- **Felt Pens are great choice for achieving bold and eyecatching designs but lack subtlety.**
- **Magic Markers or even permanent markers won't be good for colouring in this book** as they will bleed through to the underside of the paper.
- **Pencils are ideal if you prefer softer hues with a more subtle effect.** A quick look at the front cover of this book shows this: Jules has given the pencils on the left greater dimension by colouring them darker on one side. It's almost impossible to achieve effects like this with markers or crayons. On the flip side, using pencils can be slow, especially as they require regular sharpening.
- **Paint enables you to mix your own shades so is the most flexible of all media** - probably why it's been used by fine artists for centuries. However setting up paints of any kind (watecolour, gauche, acrylic or oil) is immensely time consuming. Paints require special paper or canvas too, so we wouldn't recommend using them here.

TIP: 'I swear by brush pens. They have a really fine point which makes them great for accuracy, and there's none of the mess you get with traditional paints.' **Karen**

Go with the flow

Which colours to choose?

Whilst certain colours broadly align with specific traits – red is associated with danger, purple with sophistication, brown with ruggedness and so forth – personal experiences, upbringing, cultural difference and context all add nuance to what various shades mean to us individually. We can also use colours to connect with our emotions and opt for particular shades to reflect our mood.

> TIP: *'Before I start colouring, I sharpen all my pencils. I find this this little ritual comforting – it also means I don't have to keep stopping and starting because I can't find the materials that I need to work.'* **Jules**

The rainbow method

- If you're feeling at a loss as to where to start, **you might like to begin by laying out your pens, pencils or pastels to reflect the colours of a rainbow:** red, orange, yellow, green, blue, indigo, violet.
- **First colour all the things you want to be red.** Start with the lines at the edge – this will help you to stay inside the area you're colouring. Then fill in the centre. Next colour all the things you want to be orange.
- **Continue with the rest of the colours** of the rainbow.
- **Finish by filling any remaining gaps** with intermediate or neutral colours.

When you're ready to move onto something more challenging, **you might like to watch Jules' demonstration video where she shows how to use shading and blending with pencils.** It's great fun, and you can find it in the *Making Friends with Anxiety Facebook Group,* on **julesmiller.uk** or **thecreativepumpkin.com.**

Other creative pursuits can also help alleviate anxiety

The good news is that **colouring is not the only activity to possess many of these therapeutic qualities**. There are dozens and dozens of activities that have a similar calming effect. Tapestry, for instance, also stimulates brain areas related to motor skills and entails filling in gaps with colour – it's virtually colouring-in with thread – and samples of Greek tapestry have been found dating from the third century BC. **Embroidery, patchwork, knitting, crochet – each of these forms of needlework involves playing with pattern and making creative choices with colour and thread,** and all have been with us for centuries. So perhaps colouring isn't a passing phase, but rather a connection with our ancient forebears. Certainly I know that every time I go to sleep beneath the patchwork quilt stitched by my grandmother, it's as if I can feel her spirt envelop me, even though she's long gone.

It seems no coincidence that so many of these crafts are enjoying a renaissance – not only does concentrating in this way replace negative thoughts with positive ones (you're making something – woo!), **it's a form of active meditation.** By focusing the mind on simple tasks that require repetitive motion, it creates a sense of state of peace, and many people who have a difficult time with concentrative meditation (that'll be me then) can find these sorts of activities easier.

TIP: 'A friend of mine who travels a lot has started painting tiny pictures onto pebbles she finds whilst abroad. She's several of them now, and they've become a tactile collection of memories which she keeps on her desk. When things get stressful she holds a pebble in her hand for a minute or so and visualises the place that she was when she found it – it's mindfulness, DIY-style.' **Jules**

TIP: 'When I feel anxiety rising, I try and distract myself with a craft that I enjoy.' **Polly**

'True creativity often starts when language ends.' Arthur Koestler

A balanced approach

All these pastimes activate different areas of our two cerebral hemispheres, commonly known as the left and right brain. The actions involve logic (left brain activity) as we use this to decide how to colour forms and creativity (right brain activity), which we draw upon when selecting and mixing colours. It strikes me that this is also true of Scrabble, which is both logical and creative, and maybe goes some way to explaining its perennial popularity.

TIP: *'I try to listen to my body, as if I'm exhausted it tends to make my anxiety worse. I find writing poems and singing help me relax and de-stress.'* **Marta**

TIP: *'I've always encouraged my children to try different creative pursuits. Some things they've loved (painting and baking) some things not (gardening!) but I was keen to show them that unless you give something a try, you'll never know if it's for you or not. The same goes for us adults: try before you buy into any creative pursuit, so you can see if it works for you. And hold off on spending heaps on equipment until you've done it several times and enjoyed it.'* **Jules**

Another benefit of crafts like tapestry or patchwork, say, is their flexibility – we can be as imaginative or guided by instructions as we wish. They are similar to gardening in this regard, which leads me neatly onto that very subject.

Do what makes you happy

Sowing the seeds of greater contentment

I'll come clean: when it comes to gardening, I don't plan at all. I buy flowers if I like the colour and because I like to surround myself with things I find pretty. I don't care much if plants are suited to sunshine or shade, or the soil in our tiny patio. My choices are governed by instinct, which, thinking about it in the cool light of today, is probably why only about half of what I purchase survives.

My mother, on the other hand, is more disciplined: her garden has structure. Certain plants are vetoed because the style of the foliage or horticultural heritage is found wanting. How neatly we illustrate two different approaches: I'm a 'seat-of-the-pantser'; she's a planner. And **this is one of the very best things about gardening – it accommodates all sorts of people and all levels of experience.** Any approach is fine in my book (which this is – along with Jules' – after all) as long as you **Do What Make You Happy.** And gardening can make us happy, as many a horticulturalist will testify. But why, exactly, is it such good therapy? If you're already sold on gardening, it's interesting to explore what makes it so uplifting. If you haven't done much gardening before, it might inspire you to make more space for it in your life.

TIP: 'Remember that you can't help anyone else if you don't look after yourself. Sometimes this means others may see you as selfish, but in the long run you'll be happier and healthier so try not to let what they think stop you prioritising your own wellbeing.' **Carole**

Grow yourself better

10 reasons why gardening has such a positive effect on our mental health

1. Looking after plants connects us to nature

I remember when my mum first gave me a little spot in our garden to tend; I must have been about five. I demarcated it with stones and planted forget-me-nots and 'poached eggs' – flowers that still make me smile. Having to care for plants is a good way to learn responsibility for other living things and when we are small it helps us to develop an appreciation of the magic of nature. The same is true for us as adults too – on one level, it means we can surround ourselves with plants we like aesthetically, but it goes deeper than that. Our forebears have been demarcating plots and tilling the land for millennia and **gardening connects us to something so ancient and primal it's good for the soul.**

2. Being amongst plants and flowers reminds us to live in the present moment

As I explained earlier, when we let go of ruminating on the past or worrying about the future and focus on the here and now, anxiety lessens, and one of the reasons colouring is so calming is because it allows us become more present. Gardening is similar, and can also help to lift mood. Moreover, **gardening can engage all the senses.** Next time you're in a garden or park, pause for a few moments and allow yourself to be aware of what's around you. Again, focus on your senses. Listen. Touch. Taste. Smell. See. Experiencing the fullness of nature can be very restorative.

3. **Gardening allows us all to be nurturers**

It doesn't matter if we are seven or seventy, rich or poor, plants don't give a fig who is tending them. **Horticulture is a great equalizer:** and for those with anxiety problems to be able to contribute to such a transformative activity can boost self-esteem. The impact may not be as immediate as colouring, but it's creative nonetheless.

TIP: *'I take 5 or 10 minutes to appreciate something lovely, like a nice plant or tree with the blue (or grey!) sky in the background. It's a mindfulness tool and I find it invaluable.'* **Helen**

4. **Cultivating other living things takes us out of ourselves**

Gardening serves to remind us that we are not the centre of the universe. Self-absorption can contribute to anxiety, and focusing on the great outdoors – even in the pared-down form of a patio or roof terrace – encourages us to be less insular. Yet to dig and delve in a walled or fenced garden also helps provide boundaries both literally and metaphorically, allowing us to feel safe at the same time as we expand our horizons.

TIP: *'I like to sow seeds and watch them grow into young plants, to wander around and see what has grown in overnight. To feel the earth in my hands is incredibly healing.'* **Nikki**

Never look down on someone unless you're helping them up

5. **Gardening helps us relax and let go**

For many, the peacefulness associated with gardening comes from the fact it allows us to escape from other people. 'Flowers are restful to look at. They have no emotions or conflict,' said Freud. **Tending to plants allows us to tap into the carefree part of ourselves** with no deadlines, mortgage or annoying colleagues to worry about. It's calming, again just like colouring. Moreover, the rhythm of tasks like weeding, hoeing, sowing and sweeping means thoughts can ebb and flow along with our movements. I sometimes take to watering the pots on our patio when trying to untangle knots in plotting which can arise when writing novels. Often the solution comes to me far more easily outside than if I were to continue sitting staring and despairing at my screen.

6. **Working in nature releases happy hormones**

To say that gardening encourages us to exercise and spend time outdoors is obvious, but it's worth reminding ourselves that **what's good for the body is also good for the mind.** When we exercise, levels of serotonin and dopamine (hormones that make us feel good) rise and the level of cortisol (a hormone associated with stress), is lowered. It's true that a day in the garden can leave you ready to hit the hay earlier than usual, but it can also get rid of excess energy so you sleep better and wake feeling renewed inside.

TIP: 'Remember there are lots of other people out there who are feeling similar to you, and you are not alone. Things will get better, so try to be kind to yourself until they do. Although I know that's easier said than done!' **Peter**

7. **Gardening reminds us of the cycle of life, and thus come to terms with that most universal of anxieties: death**

In the plant world, regeneration is a matter of course, but psychological repair does not necessarily come so easily to us as human beings. **Gardening is a form of ritual** involving both the giving of life and acknowledgement of its end. As such it works within our minds as a symbolic act and helps us work through difficult emotions: it's no coincidence we create gardens of remembrance and mark the scattered ashes and graves of our loved ones with roses, shrubs and trees; by doing so we're acknowledging that from dust we all come and to dust we return.

8. **Gardening allows us to vent anger and aggression**

Why beat pillows with a baseball bat or yell at the cat when you have a hedge to hack? There are times when I enjoy cutting and chopping and yanking and binding as much, if not more, than sowing and feeding and watering, and **the great thing about destructiveness in the garden is that it can be in the service** of growth – if you don't cut back plants, you will be swamped by them.

TIP: 'Mindfulness has really helped me. When I feel bad, I don't struggle against my emotions, I observe them and breathe. I try to see them as temporary feelings - like clouds floating through the sky. I'll name the emotions "anger" or "anxiety" or whatever, say "hi" and let them go.' **Philip**

Personal transformation doesn't happen overnight

9. **Gardening can be a good way of gaining a sense of control**

Anxious people often feel overwhelmed, and this can perpetuate the cycle of panic. But whereas trying to control other people is invariably a fruitless exercise, you're more likely to succeed in controlling your beds and borders.

10. **Gardening is easy**

In spite of all these benefits, the world of plants can feel intimidating to an outsider. If you're new to gardening, it's common to feel anxious you won't have green fingers, but gardening is easy if you start small and take it slow. **Don't worry if you don't have much outside space.** Just one hanging basket or a few pots along a window ledge can lift the spirits whenever you look at them, and if you're strapped for cash, why not recycle an old container like a colander or ice-cream carton? I also recommend looking for packets that say 'Ideal for Children' – who cares if you left school years ago? Nasturtiums are a good bet, as are sweet peas, or, if you can find a patch of earth which gets sunshine, try sowing sunflowers or poppies directly into the soil. **Gardening is a lot more affordable than many other forms of therapy,** so why not make an appointment with Mother Nature today?

TIP: 'I used to spend hours in the garden centre every spring seduced by the thousands of colourful seed packets from which to choose. I'd end up buying dozens – everything from poppies to petunias. Then weeks later, I'd get frustrated that I hadn't succeeded in creating the 'Chelsea Flower Show' display I'd planned in my head! This year I decided to keep it simple. I limited myself to buying only two or three packets. I chose Sweet Peas and for less than half an hour of my time in early April, I now (it's July) have bunches of pastel-petalled flowers that fill the air with glorious scent. So with gardening, keep it simple! And just like colouring, you'll very often achieve better results when you work with a limited palette! **Jules**

Similar patterns of thought

By now I hope you're beginning to see a pattern, and I don't just mean in the illustration opposite. Whilst colouring can play a great role in managing stress, **there are many, many ways to lessen the grip that anxiety holds on us.** My 'therapies' include taking photographs and sewing as they feel so different from my day job of writing; Jules loves colouring and gardening; my husband, Tom, enjoys cooking, and Jules' husband, Nic, can lose himself completely in painting and carpentry.

Of course the more we each engage in an activity the more accomplished we tend to become, but that's not what I wish to underline here: we anxious types are prone to perfectionism anyway, and all too easily can berate ourselves for not being as brilliant as we feel we should be. So quieten that inner critic if you can and get on with 'being' a colourist/photographer/gardener/cook or painter rather than 'doing' an activity. 'Doing' tends to feel like a duty and focuses on the end result; 'being' is about living in the present moment.

TIP: *'Make time to look after yourself – self-care is compulsory, not optional. By "self-care" I mean anything that you **want** to do, rather than all the stuff you think you **have** to do. Self-care is different for each of us.'* **Alistair**

I imagine one or two of you are shrugging and saying: 'I'm just not creative'. Again I beg to differ: just as everyone is anxious, everyone is creative. Yet there are plenty of other ways we can help ourselves feel calmer. You may recall I said earlier it might be an idea to channel your inner cat or dog? that's because being with animals can help alleviate anxiety, too.

TIP: *'When I'm stressed, I say to myself, "Gracie, what are you getting so wound up about? You're in competition with no one but yourself. So you're gonna win whatever!"'* **Grace**

Why spending time with our pets is so good for mental health

If you think about it for a moment, many of the therapeutic benefits of gardening are mirrored in our relationships with animals. Just as plants remind us we are not the centre of the universe, caring for another living creature can provide a positive diversion.

- Both plants and animals put us in touch with the natural world.
- Having a dog, in particular, encourages us to exercise and spend time outdoors.

But animals are good for our wellbeing in unique ways, too:

1. **Pets teach us empathy**

   Being able to imagine how animals feel can decrease the solipsism associated with anxiety. We see a dog play, we feel more playful ourselves. We hear a cat purr, we feel happier too.

2. **Pets keep us connected**

   Fundamental to maintaining a healthy mind is staying engaged with others, and pet owners often talk more readily to each other. When out walking, people with dogs will stop and chat about their pets, while the dogs socialise together – a win-win. And for those who live alone, a pet can be a lifeline.

   'There have been times that without my cats I simply wouldn't be here.' **Errol**

Being with animals is a great way to unwind

3. Pets show affection, and allow us to do the same

Having a recipient for our affections, especially a creature who responds so tangibly by wagging its tail or purring, allows us to express our own softer, more intimate side. Our pets love us unconditionally (aside from cupboard love, of course) and feeling loved is good for self-esteem.

'When I rescued my cat, she was ill and so was I. I looked after her and she took care of me just by being the very sweet, needy and loving cat she was.' **Pippa**

4. They provide us with routine

When we're down, mornings are often the hardest.

'The days I wanted to curl up and die, my dog needed to go out to toilet so he was the push I needed to get up and out. Now I'm better, I'm so thankful.' **Bill**

5. They listen without judgment, like a good therapist

What pet owner hasn't offloaded onto their pet occasionally? Obviously the insights might not be as revealing as going to a therapist, but they're great secret-keepers and there's no time limit or fee – you can talk for as long as you want.

'Just because I talk to my dog doesn't mean I'm barking!' **Jonathan**

6. Pets help us physically become calmer

Many studies have shown that having a pet helps to lower blood pressure and just stroking a cat or dog can be calming.

'I feel happy just thinking about the uncomplicated, unconditional love and joy I share with my dog on a daily basis.' **Nicola**

Be your own best friend

Time for a cuppa

Having said all this, I do realise getting a pet or taking up a creative pursuit isn't for everyone. Much of the appeal of this book doubtless comes from the opportunity it provides for colouring, and the last thing I want is to add another guilt-inducing obligation to your 'to do' list. That would only make your worry worse.

TIP: 'Realise that some days it's ok to do nothing and achieve nothing.
Because YOU are important.' **Ali**

Nonetheless, there is a one issue relating to anxiety which it can be so helpful to grasp that I don't want to end this book without touching on it. It's explained effectively by a gardening analogy, but the good news is you don't need to pick up a trowel to benefit. All I ask is that you read, and I believe your understanding of anxiety will grow, whilst at the same time the amount you're gripped by the most distressing symptoms of worry and panic will diminish. So if you need a break, make yourself a cuppa, then put your feet up and relax and I'll do my best to explain.

TIP: 'My way of overcoming anxiety is to sit with it, instead of trying to push it away,
and remind myself that I've been here before and I'm much stronger than I think.
These days, I actually say to myself, "bring it on!" when I feel anxious,
because nothing scares me in the way it used to.' **Tracey**

How to unlock the mind and be freer of anxiety

Gardeners often say a weed is **'a plant in the wrong place'**, and yesterday, when I was confronted by a mass of little yellow flowers taking over a bed I'd painstakingly planted with purple and pink pansies, it struck me that anxiety is a bit like a weed. Anxiety is a physical and mental reaction that's quite normal – all humans experience it – but in the hyper-anxious, **it's a reaction** *in the wrong place.*

A weed is perfectly natural – 'Corydalis Aurea', the fancy Latin name for the yellow flower in my garden, is not made in a factory or lab, after all. Looked at objectively, Corydalis Aurea is only doing what plants do – growing and flowering and seeding itself. It's pretty, too. Yet it upsets the colour scheme of my flowerbed, so is unwelcome.

By the same token, **anxiety is perfectly natural** – as we've seen, there's nothing wrong with anxiety per se, and at times we could actively welcome its presence as it protects us from harm. It's just that **anxiety, like a weed, can pop up when we don't want or need it; we can end up being triggered by all sorts of events and situations which shouldn't necessarily make us so worried.** In this respect anxiety is a 'habit' your body and mind has got into. The aim is to break that habit, as that's the key to feeling much better.

TIP: 'When I wobble, I remind myself: like the seasons, this too shall pass.' **Carole**

All feelings are *welcome* including anxiety

We can't avoid anxiety

In order to overcome anxiety, **it can be very tempting to think the solution is to avoid the situations that trigger it**. I've done this myself – ducking out of public speaking, foregoing parties, postponing plane trips - most of us can think of situations we've side-stepped because they scare us, and when the symptoms of excess stress and panic are so horrible, is it any wonder?

In extreme situations, fear of triggering an anxiety attack can lead sufferers to be so afraid they won't leave their own homes, as members of the *Making Friends with Anxiety Facebook Group* would testify. Yet contrary to how it might appear, this isn't because we anxious types are cowardly; it's because we're doing our best to protect ourselves against foreseeable distress. The trouble is that in the long run this doesn't help, and **by avoiding people or places we're frightened of, our worlds can end up smaller and our lives less rewarding.** In the long term most of us would prefer to break the cycle of anxious thinking but it can be hard to know how.

Let's shine a light on how this can be done using an example that many anxiety sufferers find hard: socialisng. Supposing a friend is having a party, and as you walk up the path to knock on the front door, you feel anxiety rising, begin to panic, and rush home. What happens is that your immediate anxiety will decrease, but also the message that avoidance helps to calm you begins to become hardwired into the brain. So the next time you're invited to a social gathering you feel even more filled with trepidation, and soon you're panicking every time you get an invitation.

TIP: 'Allowing yourself to feel the way you feel stops the battle which makes anxiety worse.' **Karen**

Let your inner light shine

Be gentle with yourself

The interesting thing is that if we ask ourselves what would happen if we remained in the situation we're avoiding, whilst we're convinced we'd pass out, throw up, collapse, have a heart attack or some such, actually, **after a certain time, what really happens is that anxiety begins to decrease of its own accord.** Those who've read the first *Making Friends with Anxiety* book may recall this, but I wanted to mention it again as it's so important: if we allow ourselves to ride it, eventually this anxiety passes, along with adrenaline. But we never get to learn this if we never face it. This is why it's vital to 'feel the fear and do it anyway', as the author Susan Jeffers said, as then we show ourselves we can manage the situation.

Breaking the habit of anxiety isn't something that can be done overnight or in defiance. If you challenge yourself to go to a party with 200 guests the very same day you have a job interview, you're likely to be in a state of even greater stress than usual and beat a hasty retreat. Start small and take it slow.

- **Begin with the easiest situation and practise it** – if it's socialising in large groups, start by meeting a friend for coffee.
- **Build up gradually** – if something is too hard, look at breaking it down into smaller, more manageable chunks. If going out for coffee scares you, invite a trusted friend round to your home where you'll feel more at ease.
- **Reward your achievements** – pat yourself on the back for each small step you take.
- **Don't focus on how far you've got to go** or berate yourself for not being able to face a huge gathering of strangers at once.
- **Stop before you have reached your ultimate goal.**
- **Repeat regularly,** once a day if possible, each time encouraging yourself to go a little further out of your comfort zone.
- Above all, **don't be impatient with yourself.**

'And the day came when the risk to remain tight in bud was more painful than the risk it took to blossom.' Anaïs Nin

Patience is paramount

To return to the gardening analogy, overcoming anxiety is like uprooting a dandelion. Most of us know how tricky that can be. How tempting it is to pull off the leaves with our fingers, pat over the soil and convince ourselves we've weeded rather well! But in truth this is avoiding the problem. Dandelions are nothing if not dogged, and sure as anything, the determined blighters will return to haunt you unless you do the job properly. If you're too impetuous, the chances are the root will snap off midway through the undertaking. Far better to take your time: choose a day when the soil is damp and easier to work with, get a trowel or knife and a cushion for your knees, then dig right down and gently loosen the soil from the tap root until you slowly, very slowly, prise it from the earth.

TIP: 'I've learned that it's OK to ask for help. I made a pact with myself to be honest with at least one person, instead of pretending to be OK all of the time. Accepting that it's OK not to be OK has been a big learning curve for me, and knowing that I have a support system when I'm struggling makes me feel much more comfortable.' **Rachel**

* * *

Thank you

We hope you've found this book enjoyable to read and colour, and helpful too. We'd like to thank all the members of *Making Friends with Anxiety Facebook Group*, especially those who contributed tips and advice to share with other anxiety sufferers here, and the amazing team of Admins who do their utmost to make the Facebook group such a safe space to discuss anxiety issues. If you'd like to join the group, it's open to all those over 16 – find us at **www.facebook.com/groups/makingfriendswithanxiety/** Jules and I are both members, and we look forward to meeting to you there.

You are not alone.
Find us on
Facebook and join
the conversation

www.facebook.com/groups/makingfriendswithanxiety/

About Sarah Rayner

Sarah Rayner is the author of five novels including the international bestseller, *One Moment, One Morning* and the two follow-ups which also feature her Brighton-based characters, *The Two Week Wait* and *Another Night, Another Day.*

Friendship is a theme common to all Sarah's novels, and it's a thread that connects her non-fiction titles too. Last year she published *Making Friends with Anxiety: A little self-help book to help ease worry and panic.* This was followed by *Making Friends with the Menopause: A clear and comforting guide to support you as your body changes,* in collaboration with Dr Patrick Fitzgerald and *Making Friends with Anxiety: A calming colouring book* with Jules Miller.

Sarah grew up in Richmond, Surrey and now lives in Brighton with her husband, Tom, and stepson, Sebastian. You can find her on Facebook, on Twitter and her website is **thecreativepumpkin.com.**

About Jules Miller

Before becoming a children's book author/illustrator, Jules had career as an Art Director in the advertising industry in London, which is where she met Sarah. In 2000 Jules and her young family moved from London to Brighton; Sarah moved to the seaside shortly afterwards. Four years ago Jules launched *'Jules Miller Cards',* a greetings card company which offers over 200 designs featuring her illustrations. Jules' cards now sell all over the world. In May 2013 Jules secured a two book deal with New York based publisher Sky Pony Press and her first book *Ellie and the truth about the Tooth Fairy,* was published in 2014 followed by *When Night Became Day* in 2015. You can also find Jules on Facebook and Twitter, and her website is **jules-miller.uk.**

Sarah's Books

Making Friends with Anxiety: A warm, supportive little book to help ease worry and panic

Drawing on her experience of anxiety disorder and recovery, Sarah Rayner explores this common and often distressing condition with candour and humour. She reveals the seven elements that commonly contribute to anxiety including adrenaline, negative thinking and fear of the future, and explains why it becomes such a problem for many of us. Packed with tips and exercises, this companion to mental good health draws on the techniques of Mindfulness-based Cognitive Therapy, yet reads like a chat with a friend. If you suffer from panic attacks, a debilitating disorder or just want to reduce the amount of time you spend worrying, this simple little book will give you a greater understanding of how your mind and body work together, helping restore confidence and control.

Rated 4.7*s on Amazon with 100 reviews

Rated 4.5*s on Amazon

Paperback £4.99, ebook £1.99

Paperback £6.99, ebook £1.99

Making Friends with the Menopause: A clear and comforting guide to support you as your body changes

Many women consider the menopause anything but a friend, but together with Dr Patrick Fitzgerald, Sarah Rayner explains why rathr than fighting or ignoring the changes our bodies go through, understanding the experience can help us feel a whole heap better. Just why does stopping menstruating cause such profound hormonal shifts in the body, leading us to react in a myriad of ways physically and mentally? Here you'll find the answers, along with practical advice on hot flushes and night sweats, anxiety and mood swings, muscular aches and loss of libido, early-onset menopause, hysterectomy and more, plus a simple overview of each stage of the process so you'll know what to expect in the years before, during and after.

One Moment, One Morning

'A real page-turner . . . You'll want to inhale it in one breath' **Easy Living**

The Brighton to London line. The 07:44 train. Carriages packed with commuters. A woman applies her make-up. Another observes the people around her. A husband and wife share an affectionate gesture. Further along, a woman flicks through a glossy magazine. Then, abruptly, everything changes: a man has a heart attack, and can't be resuscitated; the train is stopped, an ambulance called. For three passengers on the 07:44, life will never be the same again…

The Two Week Wait

'Carefully crafted and empathetic' **The Sunday Times**

After a health scare, Brighton-based Lou learns that her time to have a baby is running out. She can't imagine a future without children, but her partner doesn't feel the same way. Meanwhile, up in Yorkshire, Cath is longing to start a family with her husband, Rich. No one would be happier to have a child than Rich, but Cath is infertile. Could these two women help each other out?

Another Night, Another Day

'An irresistible novel about friendship, family and dealing with life's blows' **Woman & Home**

Three people, each crying out for help . . . There's Karen, worried about her dying father; Abby, whose son has autism and needs constant care; and Michael, a family man on the verge of bankruptcy. As each sinks under the strain, they're brought together at Moreland's Clinic. Here, behind closed doors, they reveal their deepest secrets, confront and console one another and share plenty of laughs. But how will they cope when a new crisis strikes?

Jules' Books

When Night Became Day

The moon is bored. He is always around the same old stars in the same old boring sky. Where's the fun in that? The sun could use a change of scenery, too, and so the moon comes up with a brilliant solution - to swap jobs! When the moon goes to work during the day, he does his best to shine, but it's simply too chilly for people to enjoy the beach. The sun doesn't manage any better. His rays make it too hot to sleep, and soon everything is in chaos. Maybe this swap isn't such a bright idea after all? *When Night Became Day* is a gentle reminder that we are all born with unique and special abilities that both children and adults will enjoy.

Ellie and the truth about the Tooth Fairy

Ellie was becoming more and more doubtful that the Tooth Fairy actually existed, convinced that it was actually grown-ups who were replacing little lost teeth with money. One day she decides to put her theory to the test, she hides her tooth under her pillow and tells nobody—except her best friend and her eavesdropping mummy…

Later that night, Ellie is awoken with a start — it's the real Tooth fairy! Together Ellie and the fairy fly across toothpaste lakes and over peppermint trees toward fairyland where an amazing secret is shared… What's more, when Ellie awakes the next morning, there's a wonderful surprise waiting, but has her adventure with the Tooth Fairy been a dream or something more?

Jules Miller Cards

Cards and prints hand finished in England

Greetings cards celebrating everything from:

- Generic Birthdays and Specific Ages
- Cats and Dogs
- Seaside and Gardening
- Good Luck and Well Done
- Christmas and Easter
- Mother's Day and Valentine's

Order online: julesmillercards.com

To commission your own personalised wedding invitations, baby announcement cards, watercolour prints and more visit:

julesmiller.uk

20343299R00039

Printed in Great Britain
by Amazon